ELLE PARTELLE

Gets Ready For School

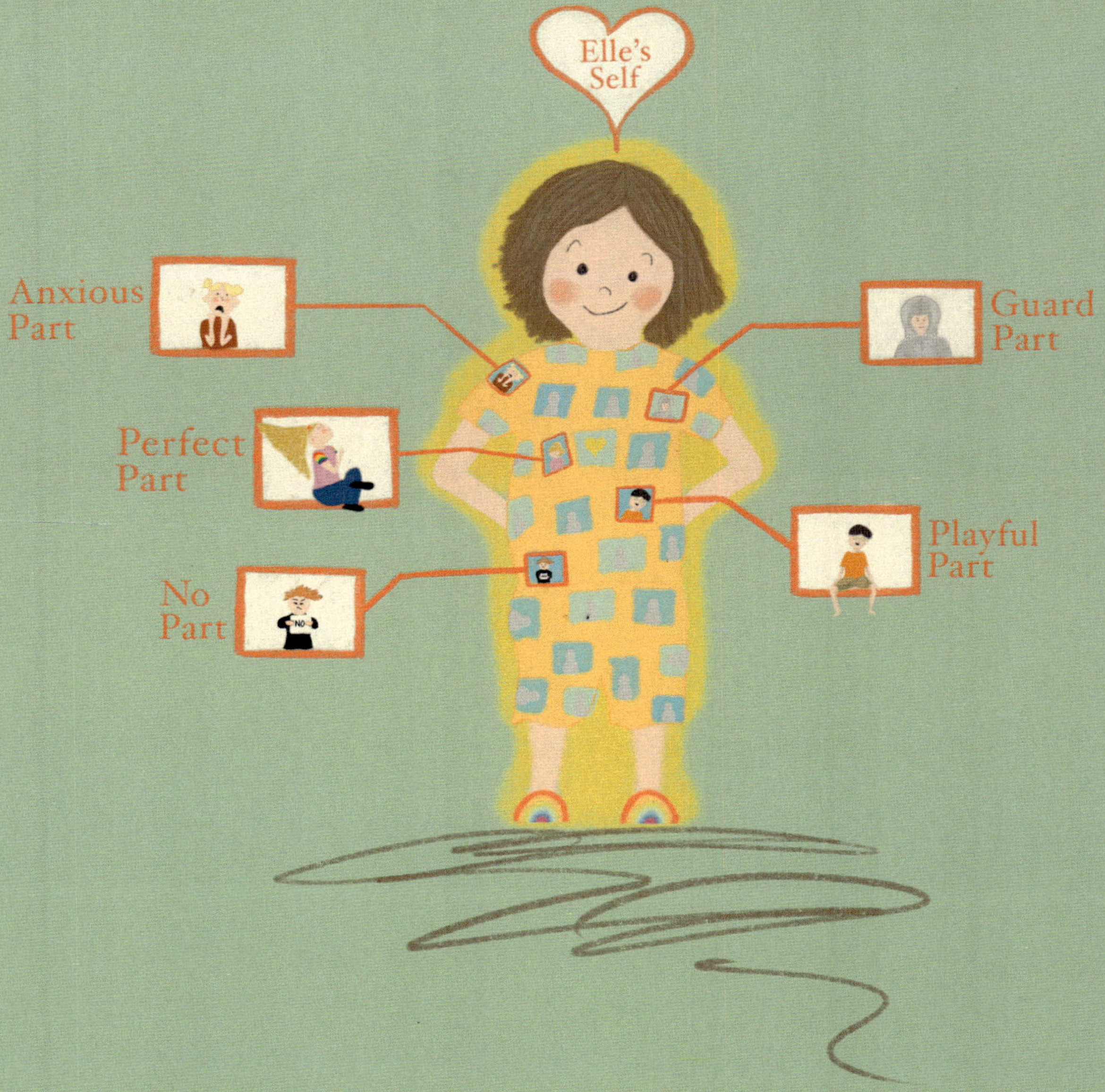

Elle's Self

Anxious Part

Guard Part

Perfect Part

Playful Part

No Part

We have an inner family of parts. Some feel good, and some feel bad. They are all trying to help us in their own way. The more we understand, listen and make space for our parts, the more we learn we are not our parts. We can get to know them, talk to them and with practice, work with them.

This book is dedicated to all who were told they are bad, lazy, dumb or else. You are good. You are made of parts who in their own way, are trying to help or distract you from getting or feeling hurt. Maybe you have a joyful part, a mean part, a wild part, a fun part and an impatient part. You have a rainbow of parts and... isn't that magical?

Copyright 2023 by Lieve de Lint - All rights reserved.

No part of this publication may be reproduced, stored in a retrieval system, or transmitted in any form or by any means, electronic, mechanical, photocopying, recording, or otherwise, without written permission of the copyright holder. Effort has been made to ensure that the information in this book was accurate and complete, however, the author and publisher do not warrant the accuracy of the information, text and graphics contained within the book due to the rapidly changing nature of science, research, known and unknown facts, and internet. Even though this book was inspired by psychological models and IFS therapy, it is not associated to any foundation or models.
The author and the publisher do not hold any responsibility for errors, omissions, or contrary interpretation of the subject matter herein. This book is presented solely for motivational and informational purposes only.

ISBN: 9789464665536

This book belongs to:

____

Elle Partelle wakes up and for a few seconds,
she feels like anything can happen.
It could be any day, week, or century.
Except it's not.
It's Monday morning, 7 a.m.
And soon, Elle's parts will wake up.

See, Elle has different parts living in her.
Each part helps Elle in its own way.

(Not always the best way).

Elle's Self can talk, manage and send love to her parts.

Sometimes..

Ten chunky caterpillars wiggle under her door: Her little brother Ben's toes.
"Go away!" yells Elle's Guard part, who jumps out of bed.
The toes wiggle.
"The door goes to MY room, so the door is MY territory!" Elle's Guard part yells.

"Good morning Guard," says Elle.
"Let's catch a breath. How are you helping me?"
"No time for breaths!" says her Guard.
"I'm protecting your space."
"Thank you," says Elle. "Can you please step aside?
I'd like to do the same, but in a friendlier way."
"Fine," says her Guard part. "But I'll stay close."

"Morning Ben," Elle says. "I need space, so I can get ready to hug you, ok?"

Ben's caterpillar toes wiggle excitedly, then tip-toe to the smell of breakfast.

Elle picks out a beautiful pair of blubber green pants.
"Yuck! My favorite color is rainbow, remember?" grumps her Perfect part.
Elle takes a different pair.
And another one.
"No, no, no," states her Perfect part.
"Rainbow sparkly dress. Rainbow boots. Rainbow everything! Way prettier."
Elle goes through all her clothes until nothing can be seen.

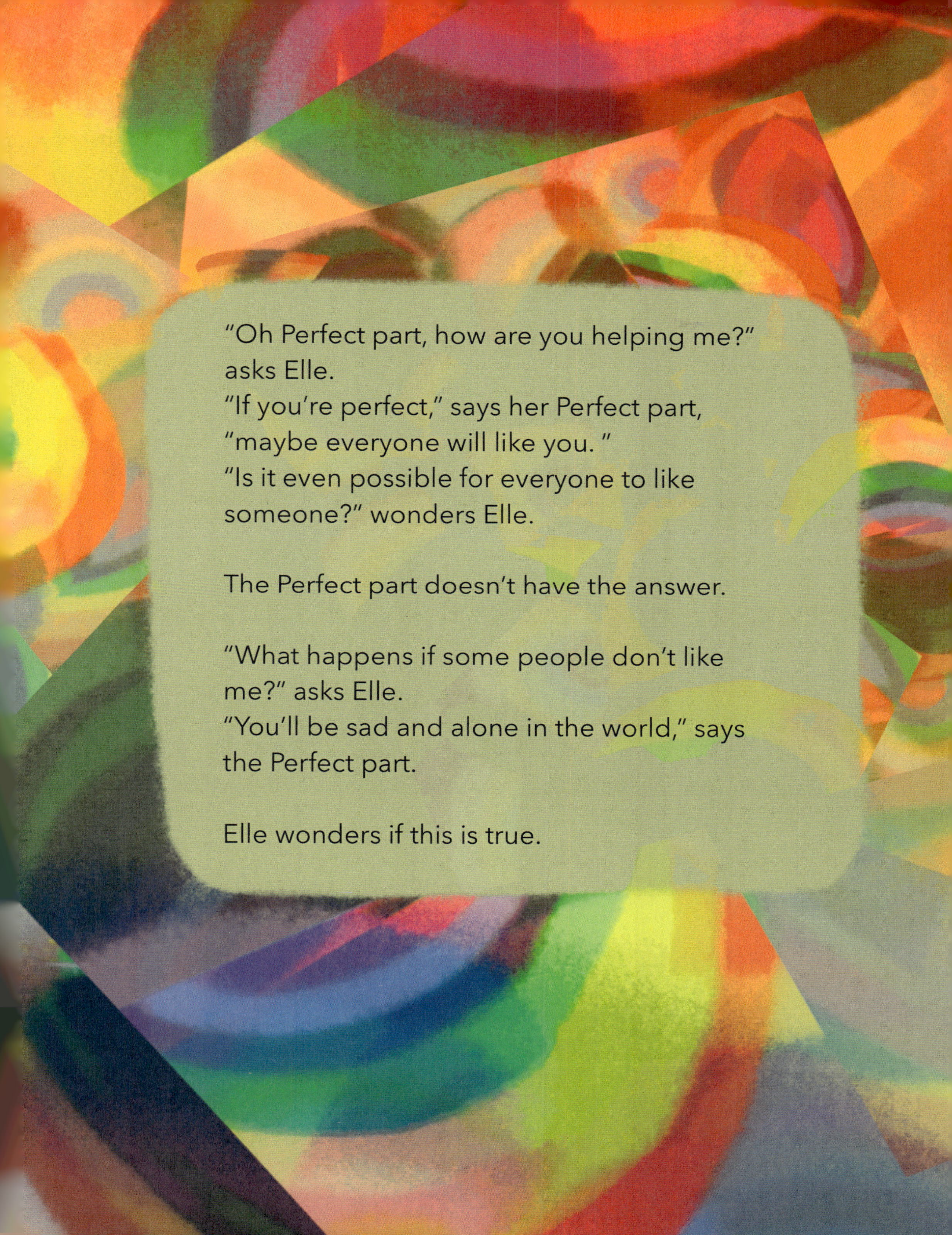

"Oh Perfect part, how are you helping me?" asks Elle.
"If you're perfect," says her Perfect part, "maybe everyone will like you."
"Is it even possible for everyone to like someone?" wonders Elle.

The Perfect part doesn't have the answer.

"What happens if some people don't like me?" asks Elle.
"You'll be sad and alone in the world," says the Perfect part.

Elle wonders if this is true.

No.

She knows a bully at school who doesn't like her even when she wears her rainbow dress.

And when she feels alone, she remembers the love of her family and friends and old Mrs. Mousetrap, her cat.

"Thanks for helping," says Elle.
"I'd like to feel beautiful and be liked too.
But now I don't like myself, or my room!"

“Psst,” goes Elle’s Playful part after some quiet.
“Remember the new climbing structure at school?
With pants, you run and hang better.
You’ll feel so free!”

“Free but not beautiful,” mumbles her Perfect part.
“Actually,” says Elle. “You both want me to feel good.
I feel beautiful in rainbow dresses. And also when I
laugh and climb a lot. So today, I’ll wear pants.”

Her Perfect part sighs, and walks away.

In the kitchen, Elle hugs Mom and Ben, carefully, because by now Ben looks like a human-size porridge.

She takes a bite of oatmeal.
"Yuck! It tastes like old bricks covered in snail slug!" says her No-part.
"I thought you liked oatmeal, at least last week?" asks Mom.
Elle thought so too.

But an Anxious part of her is also thinking of that bully at school.
And each bite of slug feels heavier.
"I'm not eating!" says her No-part.

"Oh hi," whispers Elle. "How are you helping me?"
"If you don't eat, you might not have to go to school," answers her No-part.

"Good idea," whispers Elle's Anxious part. "Because what if that bully sticks his tongue out again? We're keeping Elle safe."

"Ah," says Elle. "That was weeks ago.
I am bigger now!"
"A part of me feels scared of that boy,
but now I know to go to Ms. Bumblebelly
to ask for help. And, I like to climb!"

The next bite of oatmeal
still tastes sloppy, but ok-sloppy.

After brushing her teeth, it's time to leave.
Elle puts on her shoes until the laces become a knot.
"Not right!" says her Perfect part.
Elle tries again.

Over, under, around, and through,
Meet Mr. Bunny Rabbit, pull and through.

"Not perfect!! You can never do it.
Just stop!" orders her Perfect part.

Elle plans to throw off her shoes forever.
But then she thinks of climbing high and waving to the world upside down. She takes a deep breath.

"You again, Perfect part?" greets Elle.
"I know you're trying to help me, but I'd like to help myself in a different way. Can you step aside please?"
Her Perfect part did.

'Thank you," smiles Elle. She laces her shoes and goes out the door.

It has been a busy morning for Elle and her parts, and school hasn't even started yet.

Dear Reader,

Thank you for reading this book. I hope you enjoyed it. As an IFS-trained coach and psychologist, I am passionate about sharing stories that can help children become more in tune with their bodies and emotions in scientifically proven ways. Getting to know our parts is just the beginning of a life-long journey of self-awareness and becoming self-led. This book gives a glimpse of **how we can interact with our parts in simple story form**. It took me years to learn I am not my parts. I hope for our children this knowledge becomes a given at a younger age.

This is my second published book, and I would love to connect with you and hear what you liked and would have liked to see differently. Please send me a direct message through my website www.lievedelint.com so we can talk.

If you liked the book, **your honest review and description on Amazon would mean a lot to me and my family**. It will help get the message out there and 3% of the profit is donated to a non-profit organization helping children.

You can find the review link here: www.lievedelint.com/review-elle-partelle-gets-ready-for-school

With love and thank you,

Lieve de Lint

www.lievedelint.com

Also available on Amazon: The Anger Awareness Book

Anger can feel like a RAGING fire. How to help a child grow CALM and CONFIDENT with their BIG emotions? **"Fury Fighters to the Rescue" is a book full of evidence-based calming techniques, Fury Fighters, and anger awareness caregiver information**. Available on Amazon.

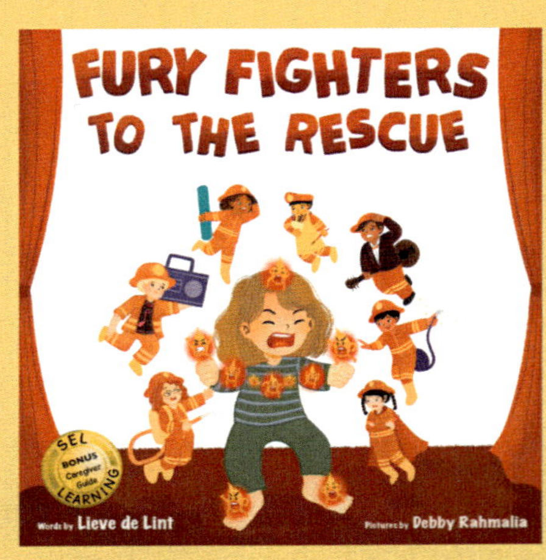

Made in the USA
Las Vegas, NV
05 April 2024

88290861R00017